Lily Beth,
    Happy adventures!
        Bridget Fancy

COOPER'S CAMPERVAN ADVENTURES
MONTANA

Written by
Bridget Farry

Illustrated by
David Globerson

To my parents, who taught and encouraged me to live a life that truly makes me happy.
And to my husband, my biggest supporter, and without whom,
life's adventures would be a lot less fun.

Published in 2025 by
Saratoga Springs Publishing, LLC
Saratoga Springs, NY 12866
www.SaratogaSpringsPublishing.com
Printed in the United States of America

ISBN-13: 978-1-955568-55-5
ISBN-10: 1-955568-54-5
Library of Congress: 2025905824
Text and illustrations Copyright © 2025 Bridget Farry

Written by Bridget Farry
Illustrations by David F. Globerson
Graphic Design by Aimee Davis
Book Design by Vicki Addesso Dodd

This book is a work of fiction. Any references to historical events, real people or
real locales are used fictitiously. Other names, characters, places and incidents
are the product of the author's imagination and any resemblance to actual events
or locales or persons, living or dead, is entirely coincidental.

All rights reserved. No portion of this book may be reproduced
or transmitted in any form or by any means, electronic, mechanical, photocopying,
recording, or by any information storage or retrieval system without written
permission from the publisher and copyright holder.
For additional information, book sales or events contact:

www.pawprintbks.com or pawprintbks@gmail.com

Dear Reader,

Hello and thank you for joining us on our adventure! I'm so glad you're here to share in the journey of Cooper's Campervan Adventures: Montana with me. This book is based on the real-life adventures our dog, Cooper, had while traveling in our campervan across the country! It's been so much fun reliving our time in Montana and getting to share it with you.

In this book, you'll meet Cooper (of course!), his papa, Matt, and his mama, Bridget (me!). The illustrations by the immensely talented David Globerson will show you all the fun we had and the beauty of Montana. Also, hidden away in two of the illustrations are the state flower, called Bitterroot, and the state butterfly, a Mourning Cloak. Please help Cooper find them!

Exploring lots of different places, and meeting so many people, has taught me a lot about the beauty of the world and the people in it, and that it's important to be kind to one another and to mother nature. I hope our story makes you want to dream big dreams, be really brave, and always believe in the magic all around you. Thank you for joining Cooper on his grand adventure. I hope you have the most magical adventures, too!

Bridget

P.S. Keep an eye out for more of Cooper's adventures yet to come!

Bitterroot

Mourning Cloak

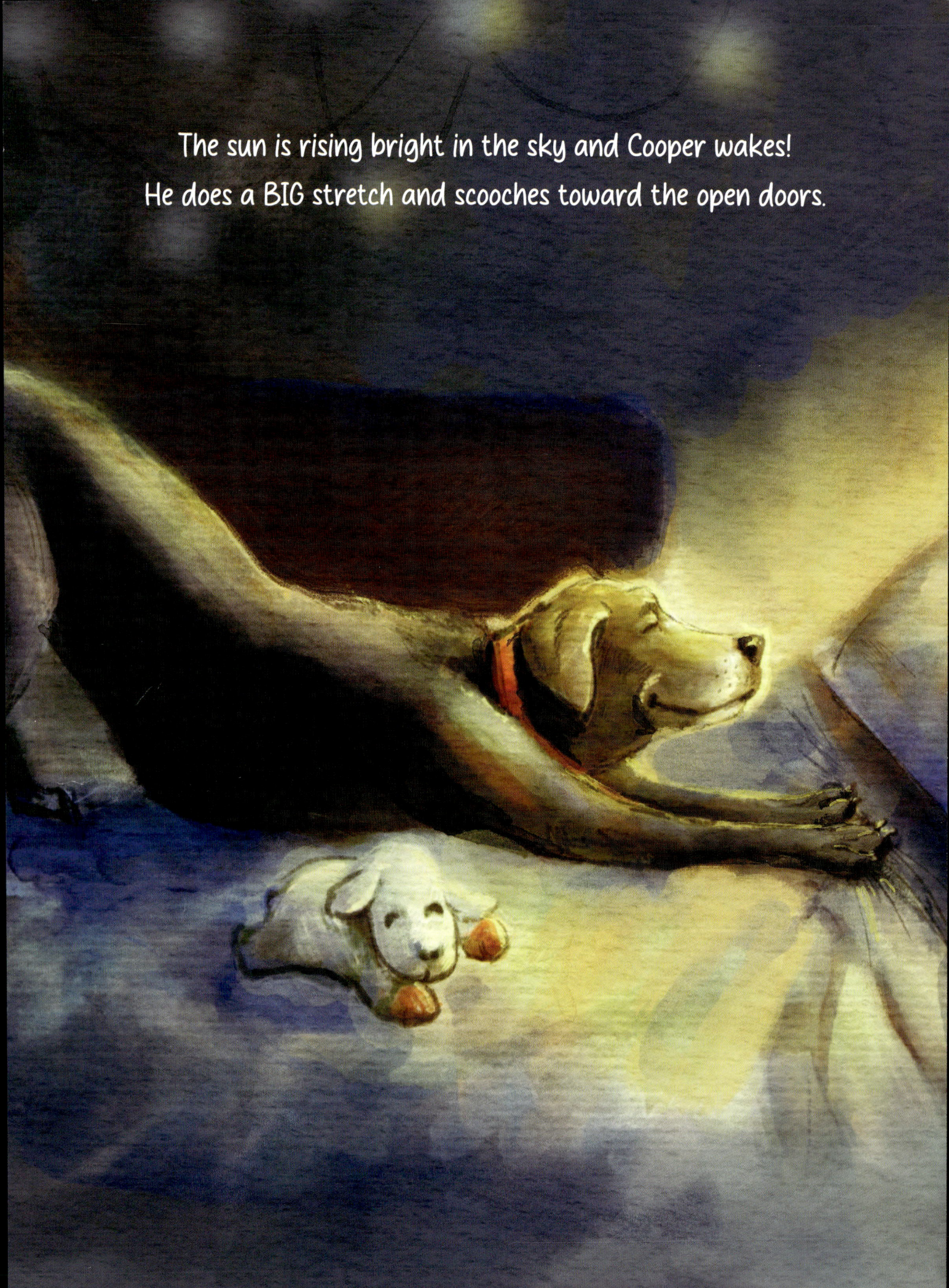

The sun is rising bright in the sky and Cooper wakes!
He does a BIG stretch and scooches toward the open doors.

His nose wiggles enthusiastically at the scents coming in from outside. A new day brings a new adventure near Glacier National Park!

What will he do with his mama and papa today?

Go swimming?

Maybe a hike like they did in Flathead National Forest?

Get to play chase with the squirrels?!

Cooper has already been having so much fun in Montana. He's hiked the towering mountains, played hide-and-seek with the squirrels, and munched on carrots while his mama and papa shopped at a farmer's market.

He even got to go to an outdoor concert in the town of Big Sky! Cooper played with a lot of new dog friends that day.

Seeing that Cooper is awake, his papa gives him his favorite good morning chin scratches while breakfast sizzles on the stove.

After breakfast, they get ready for their next adventure!

His papa takes out the
paddle boards AND fishing poles.
"Woof! Woof!" Cooper says excitedly.
His mama laughs. "I know, Coop!
Two of your favorite things!"

Cooper loves this time because he gets to look for sticks in the water, which he brings back to shore to chew on. With each stick rescue, Cooper does a big shake. The water is quite chilly! BRRR!

Next, they hop on the paddle boards to explore the glacial river. In the distance they spot a grizzly bear in the forest and quietly float by. They don't want to disturb the bear and her cubs. Shhhh.

Moments later, they see a moose and Cooper's favorite – a squirrel! He does happy tippy-taps. He wants to swim ashore to play, but his mama smiles and says, "I think they're enjoying their own game right now, Coop! You can swim to shore later…"

As they paddle, he listens to his mama and papa talking excitedly about the bighorn sheep and elk they spotted yesterday. He smiles, remembering how amazing they were!

When they return to shore, they make sure to pack up all of their belongings. Cooper has learned to leave no trace that they were ever there. That way, the river and forest can stay as beautiful as they were for him today.

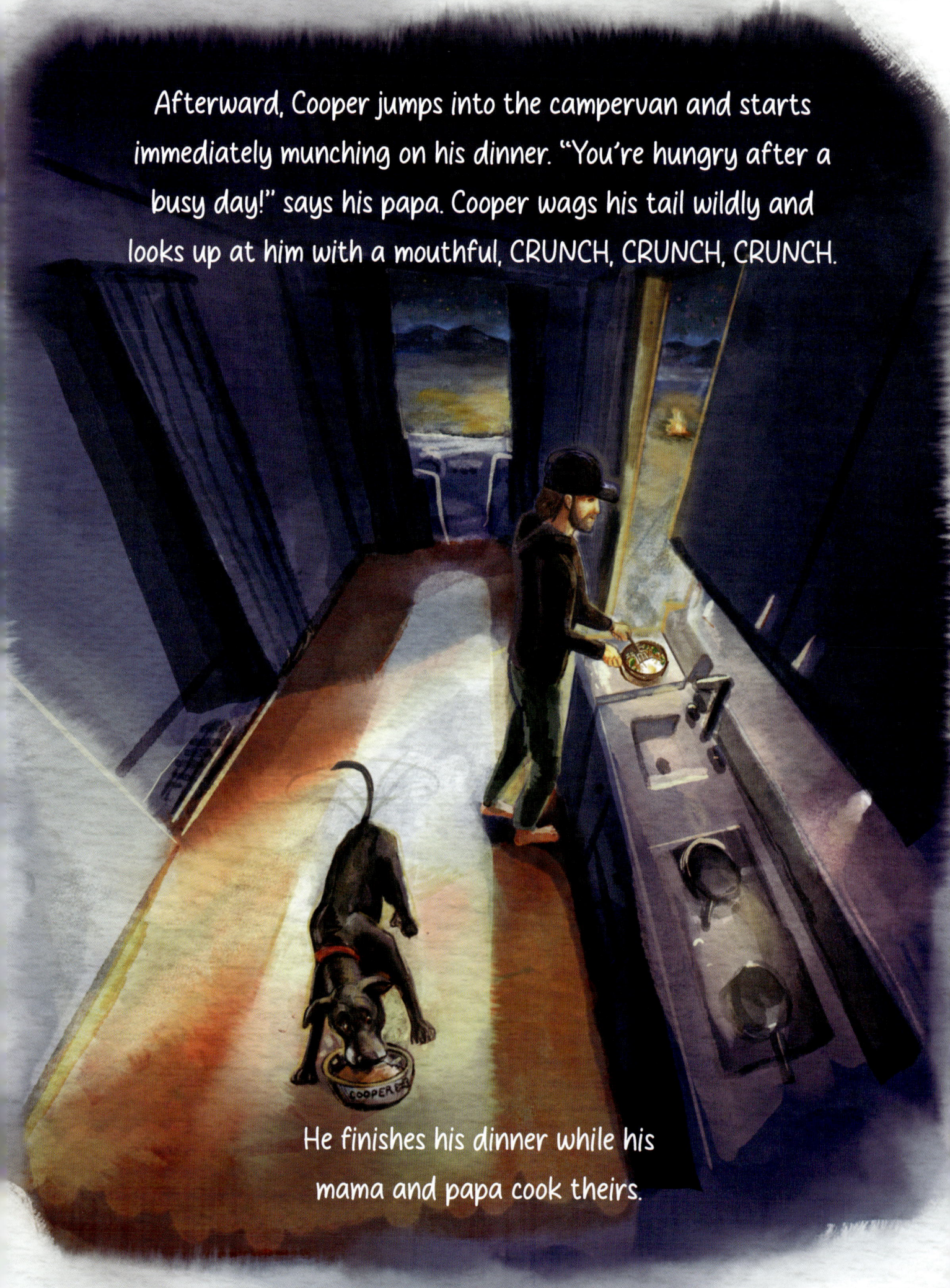

Then, he waits politely, hoping his mama will sneak him a piece of chicken.

And YES, she does!

Ready for bed, Cooper picks up his favorite toy, Lambie, who makes a squueeeak as he climbs in to cuddle with his mama and papa. He lets out a big, cozy sigh as his mama scratches his ears gently. Aaahhh.

He then drifts happily off to sleep dreaming of what adventure awaits them tomorrow.
Sweet dreams, Cooper!

About the Author

Bridget Farry was born and raised in Saratoga Springs, New York. As a child, she was always drawn to nature, and the time she spent in it sparked a much wider curiosity to someday see more of the world. Now, she, her husband Matt, and their dog, Cooper, spend their time doing just that. She's often asked what her favorite place is that she's visited. While she can't choose just one, she does have some favorites: Mountains? North Cascades. Big city? New York. Wildlife spotting? Alaska. Travel buddies? Matt and Cooper! So, inspired by her mom to write a children's book, she hopes the stories she shares of their adventures will encourage the kids who read them to discover their favorites, too.

About the Illustrator

Dave Globerson is a graduate of the Hartford Art School and a native of upstate New York. He has spent over a decade creating custom artwork for clients, friends and family. From pet portraits to fantasy worlds, Dave's work spans watercolor, acrylic, and digital painting, as well as bringing Cooper's adventures to life through his illustrations. What started as small commissions during the pandemic, has grown into a full-time career, fueled by the joy that art brings to others. Whether it's a heartfelt tribute, a whimsical character, or something entirely new, Dave loves turning imagination into reality!

About Cooper

Cooper is a rescue dog who was adopted in July of 2017. He is a sweet, funny guy who is a bit shy when he meets new people. But once he gets to know you, he is your very best friend. Cooper is always up for an adventure and takes every opportunity to cuddle. His favorite place is the beach, but when it comes to treats, he'd have a hard time picking just one. His top contenders would likely be cheese, chicken and doggie ice cream! But his favorite of all things is being with his favorite people, who love being with him, too.